DIY JEWELRY

PARACORD

Grab some cool paracord in your favorite colors and get started making hot bracelets and other accessories to wear and share with friends! We make it easy, with no special tools required. Tied in interesting knots and sometimes accented with beads, this super-strong nylon cord makes a bold fashion statement. The simple lessons begin on page 6, with beginner projects featuring each type of knot.

LEISURE ARTS, INC.
Maumelle, Arkansas

CONTENTS

THINGS YOU NEED TO KNOW 4

COBRA STITCH KNOT 6

TRILOBITE KNOT 20

CHAIN SINNET KNOT 30

STITCHED SOLOMAN BAR KNOT 34

RAISING THE BAR KNOT 40

HOW TO TIE A DIAMOND KNOT 46

THINGS YOU NEED TO KNOW

WHAT KIND OF PARACORD TO USE

All the projects in this book are made with 550 paracord. The instructions in this book are based on 18' hanks, but you may not use the whole hank for a project.

When cut lengths are given in the project instructions, the lengths always includes a little extra cord—it's better to have too much than to run short. When no cut lengths are given, you will need the entire 18' length.

OTHER SUPPLIES YOU WILL NEED

One of the great things about paracord crafting is you don't need a lot of supplies. With just some cord, utility scissors, and a ruler, you can make a bracelet. Or, add a side-release buckle to make a buckled bracelet. Tape (masking, painter's, or duct) is useful for securing cords while you tie the knots.

HOW TO SIZE A BRACELET

Measure your wrist *(Fig.1)* and decide how loose you want your bracelet. This measurement is your finished bracelet size.

Fig. 1

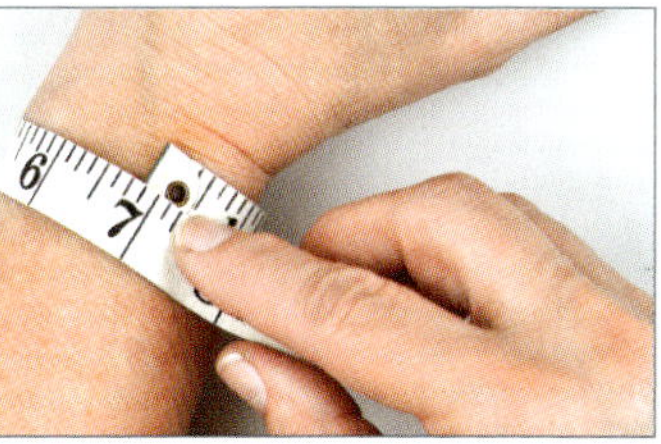

HOW TO TRIM AND FINISH

Cord ends should be coated with craft glue and allowed to dry when you cut a cord into lengths, anytime you finish using a cord and the trim the ends, or as directed in the project instructions.

Trim the cord with sharp utility scissors. When you trim the cords, allow at least 1/4" of cord for gluing *(Fig. 2)*. Apply a generous amount of glue to the cut ends and allow to dry.

Fig. 2

SOME KNOTTY TERMS

Working cord(s) or working end(s) refers to the cord(s) or cord end(s) in use.

Standing cord(s) refers to the cord(s) not being used to tie or that are secured to your work surface.

"Right cord" or "left cord" refers to the position of the cords as they face you when you are knotting unless otherwise noted in your project instructions.

COBRA STITCH KNOT

ONE COLOR BRACELET WITH LOOP AND KNOT

Shown in gold on page 6.

SHOPPING LIST

- ☐ 550 paracord – one 18' hank
- ☐ utility scissors
- ☐ tape measure, ruler, or yardstick
- ☐ craft glue
- ☐ masking, painter's, or duct tape

Tip: *Taping down the top loop and the standing cord ends makes it easier to tie knots around the standing cords.*

1. Cut an 11' length of cord for the working cords and and a 5' length of cord for the standing cords.

2. Fold the standing cord in half and center it on the working cord ***(Fig. 1)***.

Fig. 1

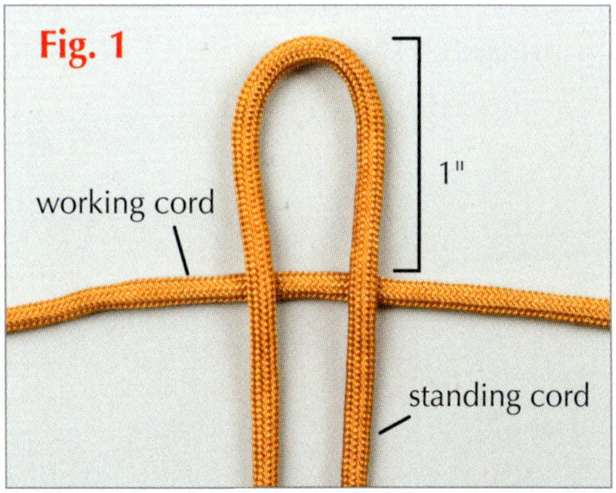

3. Knot the working cord onto the standing cord as shown in **Fig. 2**; pull the working cords to tighten.

Fig. 2

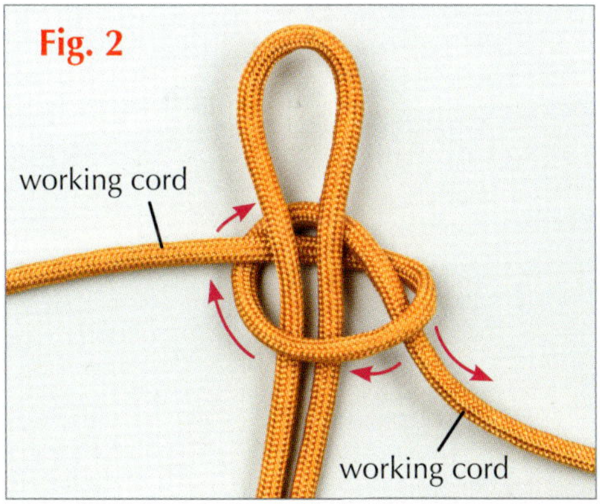

Continued on page 8.

Cobra Stitch Knot continued.

4. Follow **Figs. 3-4** to tie a Cobra Stitch knot, tightening the cords between the steps.

Fig. 3

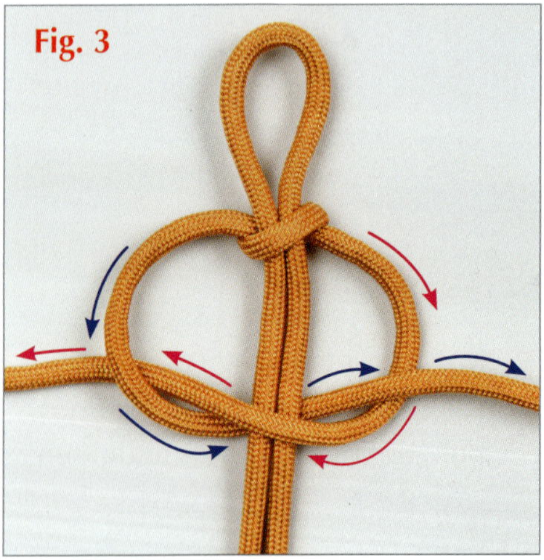

Fig. 4

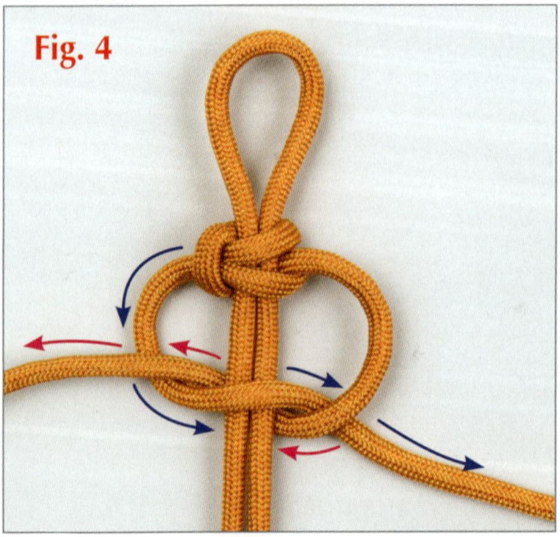

5. Repeat Step 4, stopping when the knotted section is 1" short of your finished bracelet size.

6. On the wrong side, thread the working cords under the last knot ***(Fig. 5)***; tighten. **Trim and Finish** *(page 5)* the ends.

Fig. 5

7. Use the standing cords to make a **Diamond Knot** *(pages 46-48)*.

ONE COLOR BRACELET WITH BUCKLE

Shown in green on page 6.

SHOPPING LIST

- ☐ 550 paracord – one 18' hank
- ☐ side-release buckle
- ☐ utility scissors
- ☐ tape measure, ruler, or yardstick
- ☐ craft glue
- ☐ masking, painter's, or duct tape

***Tip:** Taping down the buckle pieces makes it easier to tie knots around the standing cords.*

1. Fold the cord in half and insert the loop through one buckle piece from front to back. Bring the cords through the loop ***(Fig. 6)***; pull the cords to tighten.

Fig. 6

Continued on page 10.

Cobra Stitch Knot continued.

2. Thread the cord ends through the remaining buckle piece and position the buckle at your finished bracelet size ***(Fig. 7)***.

3. Follow Steps 4-5 of **One Color Bracelet With Loop And Knot** *(page 8)* to tie a series of **Cobra Stitch** knots ***(Fig. 8)***, ending at the beginning buckle.

Fig. 7

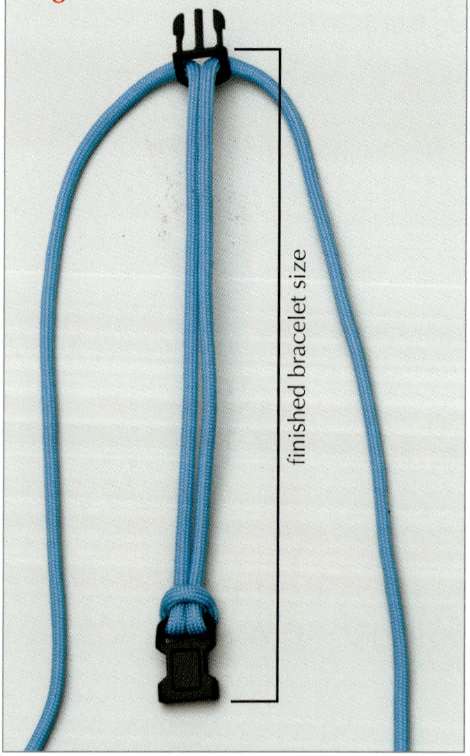

Fig. 8

4. On the wrong side, thread the working cord ends under the last knot ***(Fig. 9)***; tighten. **Trim and Finish** *(page 5)* the ends.

Fig. 9

TWO COLOR BRACELET WITH BUCKLE

Shown in blues on page 6.

SHOPPING LIST

- ☐ 550 paracord – one 18' hank **each** of two colors
- ☐ side-release buckle
- ☐ utility scissors
- ☐ tape measure, ruler, or yardstick
- ☐ craft glue
- ☐ masking, painter's, or duct tape

Tip: *Taping down the buckle pieces makes it easier to tie knots around the standing cords.*

1. Cut a 12' length of **each** cord color.

2. Insert about 2" of each cord through one end of the buckle. Secure the ends to the cords with narrow pieces of tape ***(Fig. 10)***.

Fig. 10

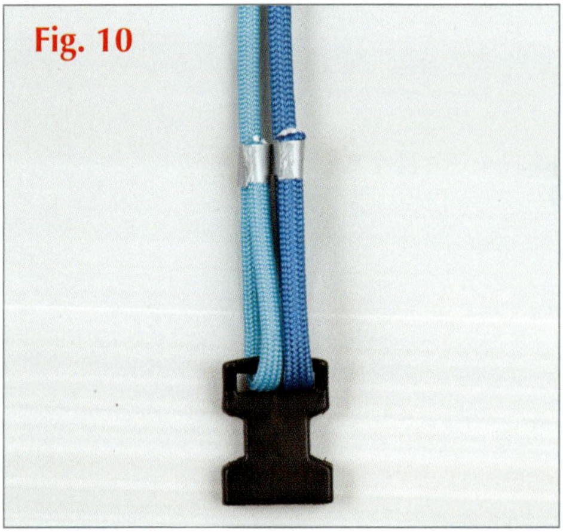

3. Thread the cord ends through the remaining buckle piece and position the buckle at your finished bracelet size ***(Fig. 11)***.

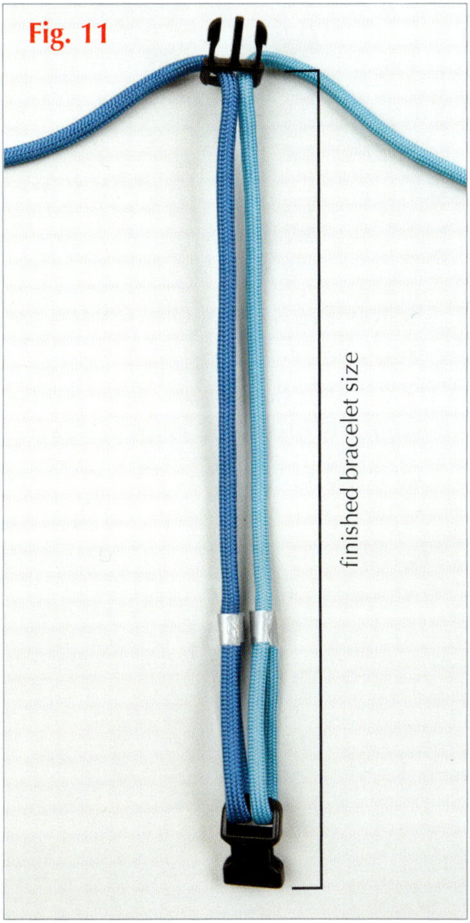

Fig. 11

4. Follow Steps 4-5 of **One Color Bracelet With Loop And Knot** *(page 8)* to tie a series of **Cobra Stitch** knots, ending at the beginning buckle.

5. Follow Step 4 of **One Color Bracelet With Buckle** *(page 11)* to finish your bracelet.

BEADED BRACELET WITH BUCKLE

SHOPPING LIST

- ☐ 550 paracord – one 18' hank
- ☐ side-release buckle
- ☐ 3 large-hole, metal-lined glass beads
- ☐ utility scissors
- ☐ tape measure, ruler, or yardstick
- ☐ craft glue
- ☐ masking, painter's, or duct tape

Tip: *Taping down the buckle pieces makes it easier to tie knots around the standing cords.*

1. Cut an 18" length of cord. Insert about 2" of the cord through one end of the buckle. Secure the cord end with a narrow piece of tape. Insert the remaining cord through the buckle ***(Fig. 12)*** and align the long ends.

Fig. 12

2. Follow Steps 4-5 of **One Color Bracelet With Loop And Knot** *(page 8)* to tie 5 **Cobra Stitch** knots. Slide a bead on the center cord and tie another knot ***(Fig. 13)***.

Fig. 13

3. Slide another bead on the center cord, tie another knot, and slide the last bead on the center cord. Tie 5 more knots. You can make the bracelet longer or shorter by tying more or less knots at the end.

4. Slide the remaining buckle piece on the cords. Follow Step 4 of **One Color Bracelet With Buckle** *(page 11)* to finish your bracelet, threading the center cord under the last knot with the working cords.

HEADBAND

SHOPPING LIST

- ☐ 550 paracord – one 18' hank **each** of two colors
- ☐ headband
- ☐ utility scissors
- ☐ tape measure, ruler, or yardstick
- ☐ craft glue

1. Use a generous amount of craft glue to adhere one cord end of each color to the inside of the headband at one side ***(Fig. 14)***.

Fig. 14

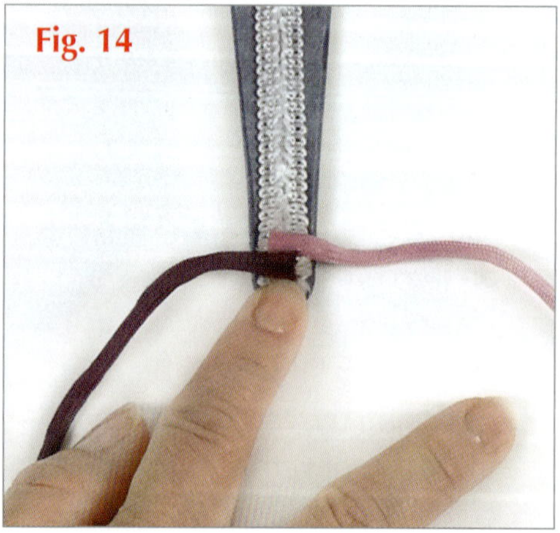

2. Follow Steps 4-5 of **One Color Bracelet With Loop And Knot** *(page 8)* to tie a series of **Cobra Stitch** knots on the headband, ending at the opposite end of the headband.

3. On the wrong side, thread the cord ends under the last knot ***(Fig. 9, page 11)***; tighten. **Trim and Finish** *(page 5)* the ends.

FLIP FLOPS

SHOPPING LIST

- ☐ 550 paracord – one 18' hank **each** of two colors
- ☐ flip flops
- ☐ utility scissors
- ☐ tape measure, ruler, or yardstick
- ☐ craft glue

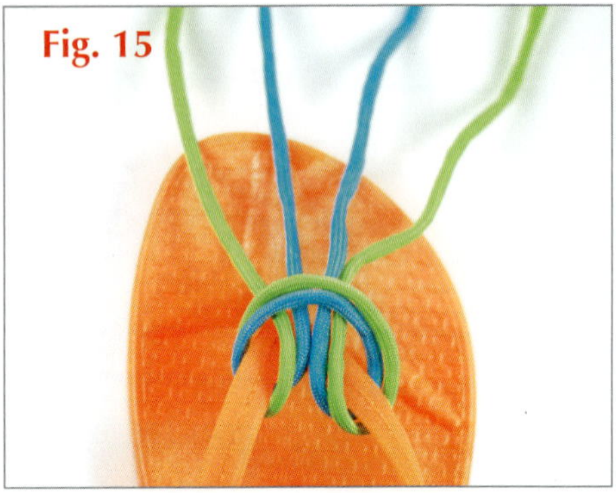

Fig. 15

1. Cut each hank of cord in half.

2. Place the center of one of each cord color over a flip flop toe piece. Pull the cord ends around the toe piece and back through the loops ***(Fig. 15)***; tighten. Pull one end of each color to each side of the flip flop.

3. Follow Steps 4-5 of **One Color Bracelet With Loop And Knot** *(page 8)* to tie a series of **Cobra Stitch** knots on one strap, ending at the opposite end of the strap ***(Fig. 16)***.

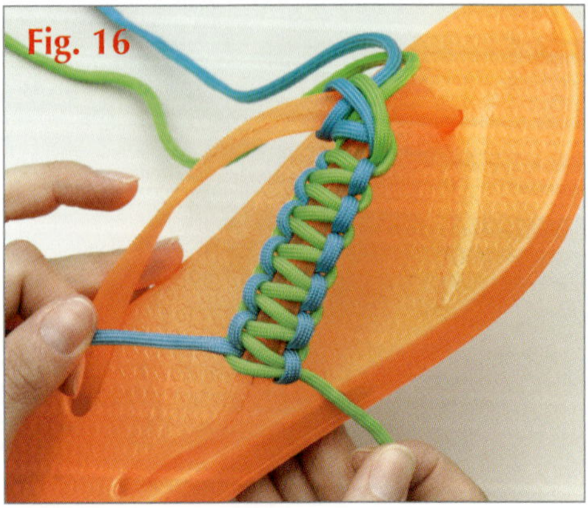

Fig. 16

4. On the wrong side, thread the cord ends under the last knot ***(Fig. 17)***; tighten. **Trim and Finish** *(page 5)* the ends.

5. Repeat Steps 3-4 on the other strap.

6. Repeat Steps 2-5 with the remaining cord and flip flop.

TRILOBITE KNOT

TWO COLOR BRACELET WITH LOOP AND KNOT

Shown in red with black and light grey with black multi on page 20.

SHOPPING LIST

- ☐ 550 paracord – one 18' hank **each** of two colors
- ☐ utility scissors
- ☐ tape measure, ruler, or yardstick
- ☐ craft glue
- ☐ masking, painter's, or duct tape

Tip: *Taping down the top loop and the standing cord ends makes it easier to tie knots around the standing cords.*

1. Holding one cord of each color together, fold the cords in half and tape the center loop to your work surface.

2. ***Note:*** *You will be working towards the beginning loop.* Using 1 working cord of each color, begin knotting at your finished bracelet size minus 1" ***(Fig. 1)***.

Fig. 1

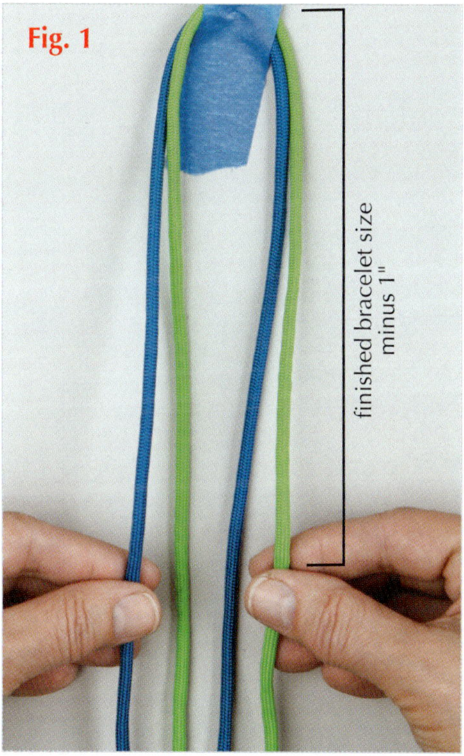

Continued on page 22.

Trilobite Knot continued.

3. Bring the right working cord over the standing cords and under the left working cord ***(Fig. 2)***.

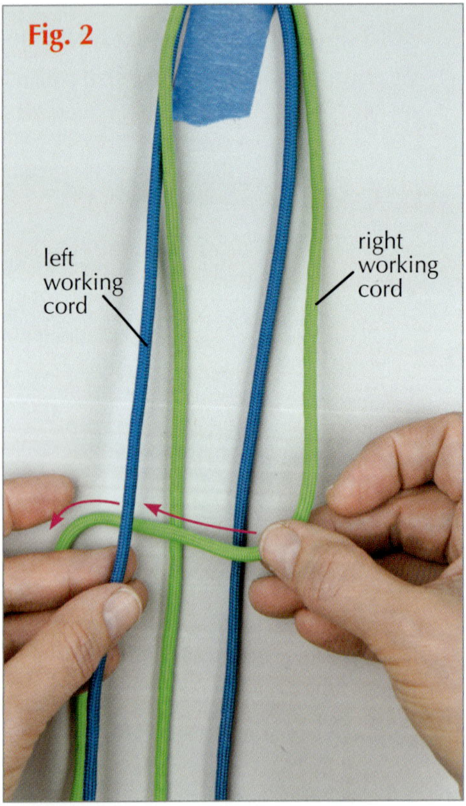

4. Bring the left working cord under the standing cords and over the right outer cord ***(Fig. 3)***; pull the working cords to tighten.

Tip: *The cord passing from right to left always crosses over the standing cords and the one passing from left to right always crosses under the standing cords.*

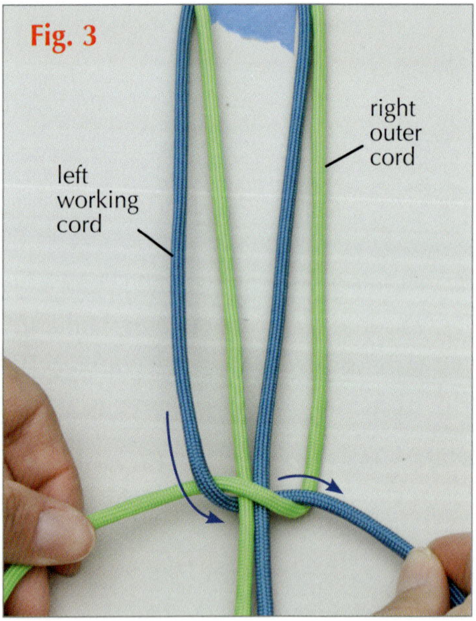

5. Bring the right working cord under the right outer cord, over the standing cords, and under the left outer cord; do not tighten ***(Fig. 4)***.

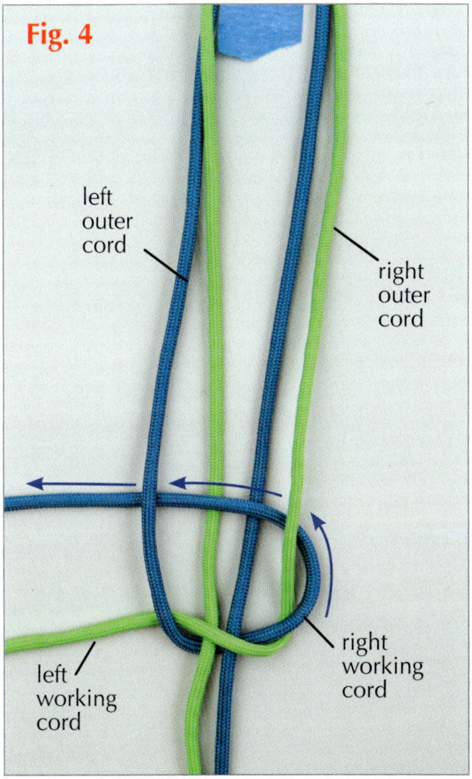

Fig. 4

6. Bring the left working cord over the left outer cord, under the standing cords and over the right outer cord ***(Fig. 5)***; pull the working cords to tighten.

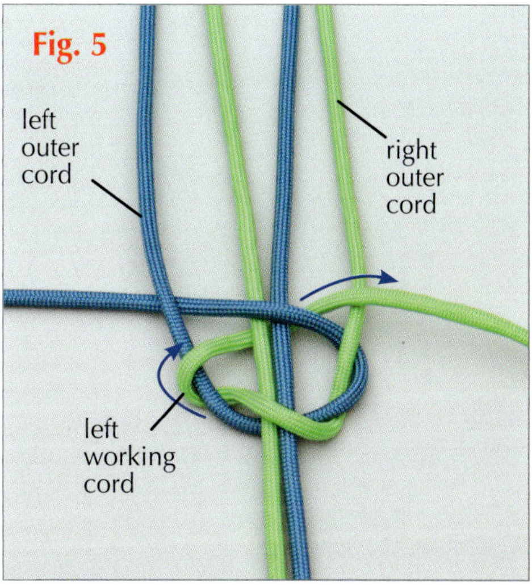

Fig. 5

Continued on page 24.

Trilobite Knot continued.

7. Repeat Steps 5-6 ***(Figs. 6-7)*** until the knotted section is 1" short of the beginning loop.

Fig. 6

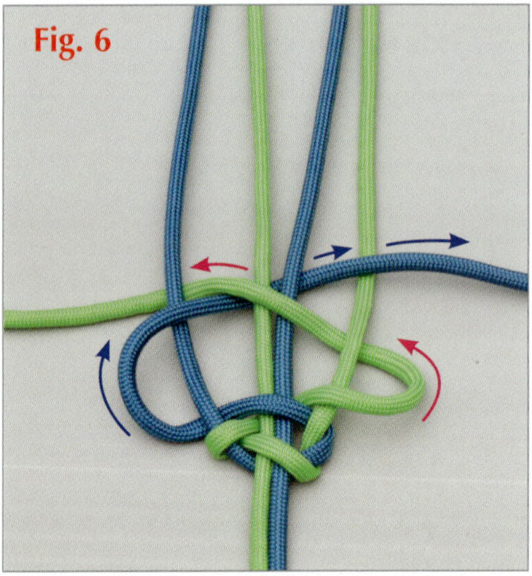

Fig. 7

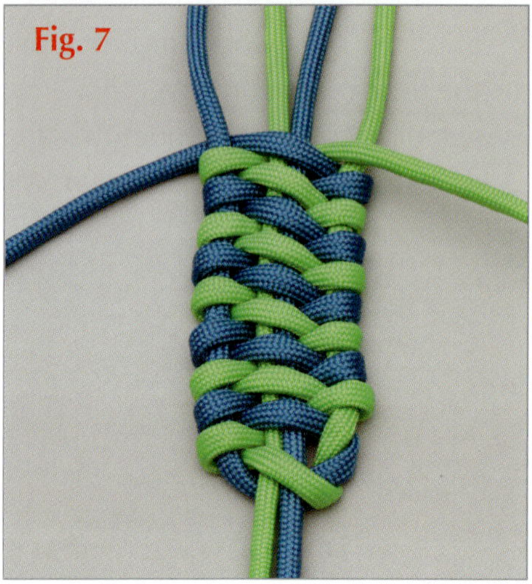

8. On the wrong side, thread the working cords under the last two knots ***(Fig. 5, page 8)***; **Trim and Finish** *(page 5)* the ends.

9. Use the standing cords to make a **Diamond Knot** *(pages 46-48)*.

ONE COLOR BRACELET WITH BUCKLE

Shown in purple on page 20.

SHOPPING LIST

- ☐ 550 paracord – one 18' hank
- ☐ side-release buckle
- ☐ utility scissors
- ☐ tape measure, ruler, or yardstick
- ☐ craft glue
- ☐ masking, painter's, or duct tape

***Tip:** Taping down the buckle pieces makes it easier to tie knots around the standing cords.*

1. Cut a 13' and a 3' length of cord.

2. Fold both cords in half and insert the 3' cord through the lower buckle opening and the 13' cord through the upper buckle opening from front to back ***(Figs. 8-9)***.

Fig. 8

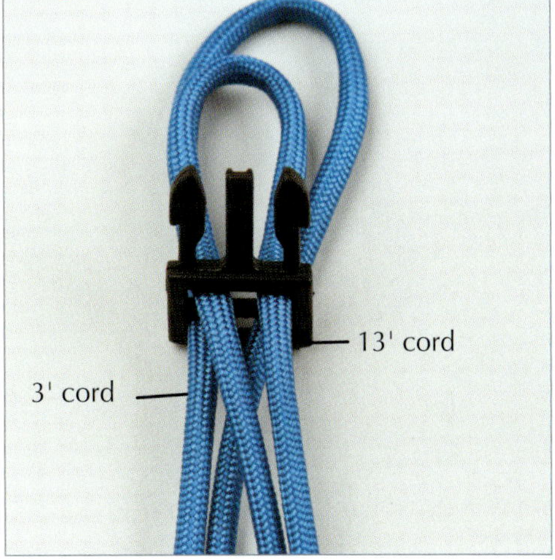

Fig. 9

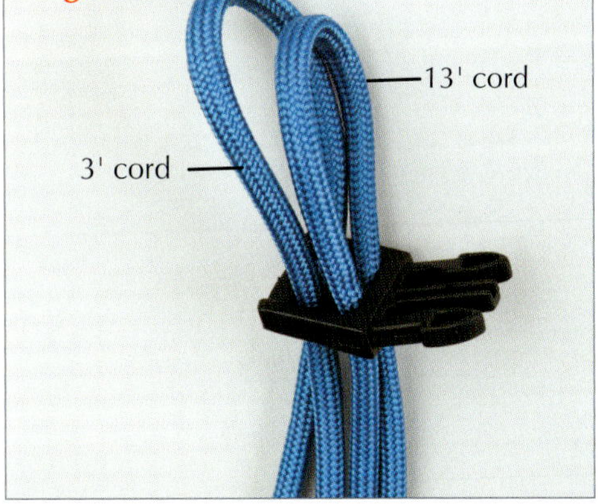

Continued on page 26.

Trilobite Knot continued.

3. Bring all four cord ends through both loops and tighten ***(Figs. 10-11)***.

Fig. 10

Fig. 11

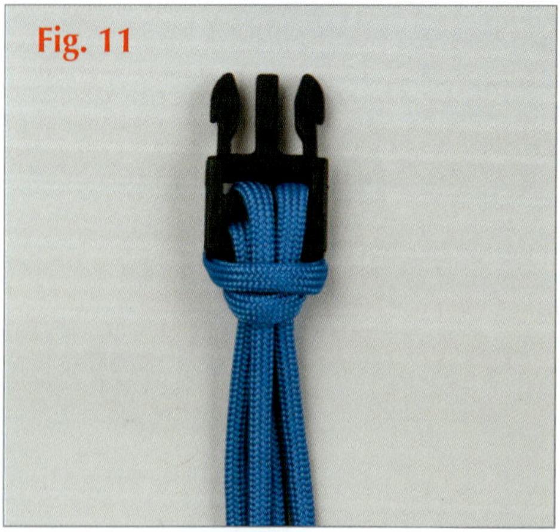

4. Keeping the shorter cords in the center, thread all four cord ends through the other buckle piece from front to back and position the buckle at your finished bracelet size ***(Fig. 12)***.

Fig. 12

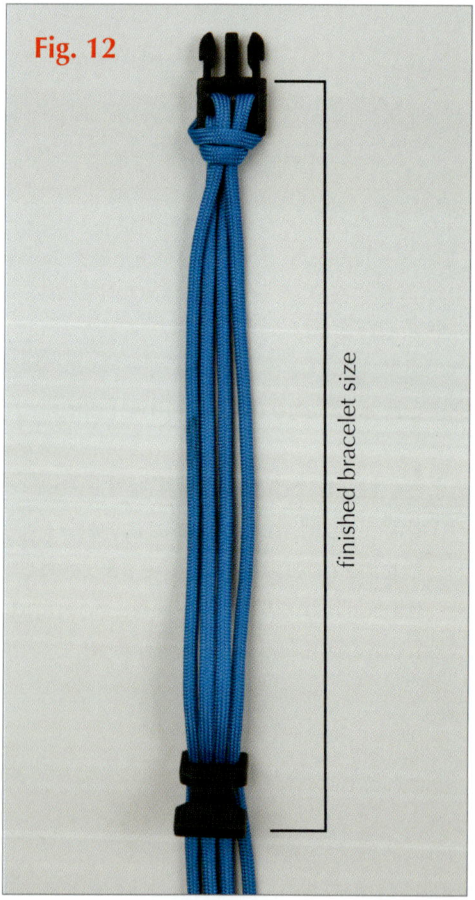

5. To join the short cord ends to the short cords, fold each short cord end to the wrong side and leaving about 2" from buckle to ends, trim the short cords. Use narrow pieces of tape to secure the ends to the corresponding cords ***(Fig. 13)***.

Fig. 13

6. With the right side facing you, cross the working cords behind the standing cords ***(Fig. 14)***.

Fig. 14

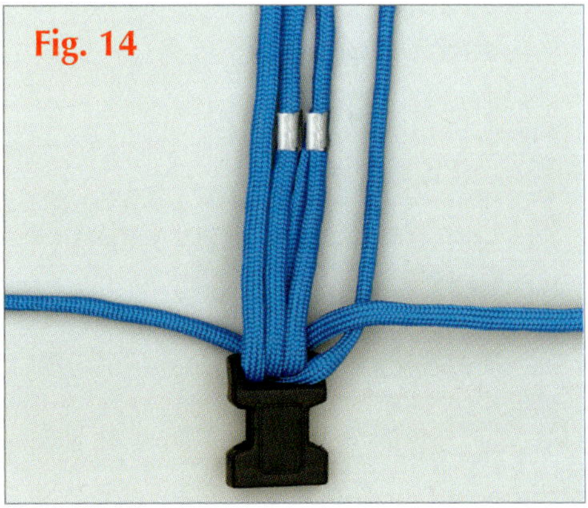

7. Follow Steps 5-7 of **Two Color Bracelet with Loop And Knot** *(pages 23-24)* to tie a series of **Trilobite** knots until you reach the beginning buckle.

8. On the wrong side, thread the working cords under the last two knots ***(Fig. 9, page 11)***; **Trim and Finish** *(page 5)* the ends.

KEY FOB

Approximate finished length: 3"

SHOPPING LIST

- ☐ 550 paracord – one 18' hank **each** of two colors
- ☐ $1^{1}/_{4}$" metal split ring
- ☐ utility scissors
- ☐ tape measure, ruler, or yardstick
- ☐ craft glue
- ☐ masking, painter's, or duct tape

***Tip:** Taping down the ring makes it easier to tie knots around the standing cords.*

1. Cut a 3' length of each cord color.
2. For the standing cords, fold 12" of each cord over the split ring.
3. Using the two longer cords as the working ends, follow Steps 2-7 of **Two Color Bracelet with Loop and Knot** *(pages 21-24)* working until you reach the split ring.
4. On the wrong side, thread the working cords under the last two knots ***(Fig. 5, page 8)***. Tuck the standing cord ends under the first two knots on the opposite side. **Trim and Finish** *(page 5)* the ends.

CHAIN SINNET KNOT

BRACELET

SHOPPING LIST

- ☐ 550 paracord (one 18' hank will make 2 bracelets)
- ☐ utility scissors
- ☐ craft glue
- ☐ tape measure, ruler, or yardstick

***Note:** This bracelet does not open and close with a loop and knot or a buckle, so it needs to be loose enough to slip on and off your hand.*

1. Cut an 8' length of cord.

2. Make a loop in the center of the cord. Wrap the right cord around the loop and bring the end under the wrap. Pull the cords to make a loose knot; do not over-tighten. The left cord becomes the sliding cord ***(Figs. 1-2)***.

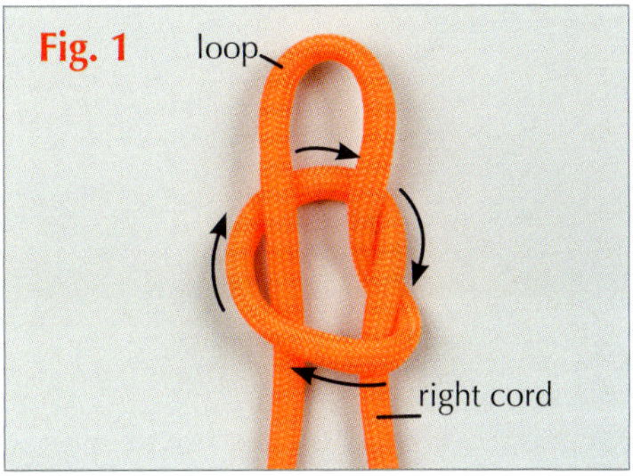

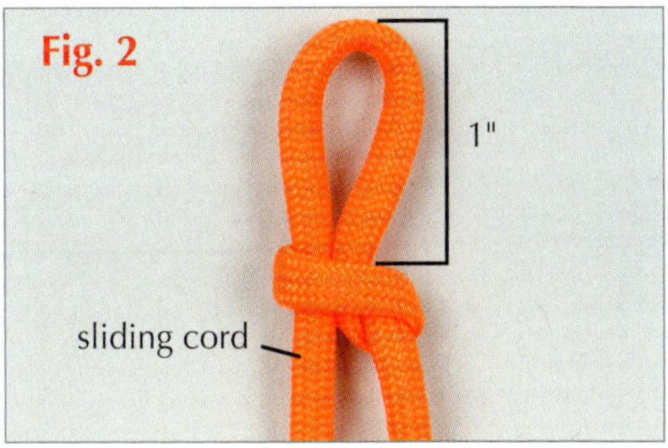

3. Turn the cords so that the sliding cord is on the right. Fold the left cord and insert the fold through the loop ***(Fig. 3)***.

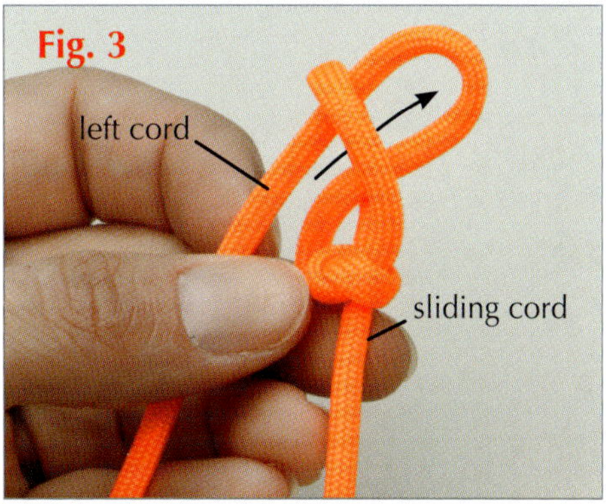

4. Pull the sliding cord to tighten ***(Fig. 4)***.

Continued on page 32.

Chain Sinnet Knot continued.

5. The cord on the left is now the sliding cord. Insert the folded right cord into the loop and tighten ***(Figs. 5-6)***.

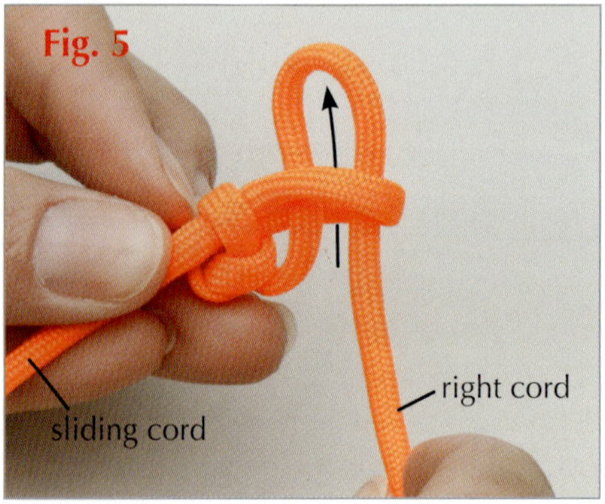

6. Continue making loops, alternating left and right cords until the bracelet is the right size ***(Fig. 7)***.

7. To close the bracelet, open the first loop by tugging on it ***(Fig. 8)***. Insert the last loop made into the opened loop ***(Figs. 9-10)***.

Fig. 8

Fig. 9

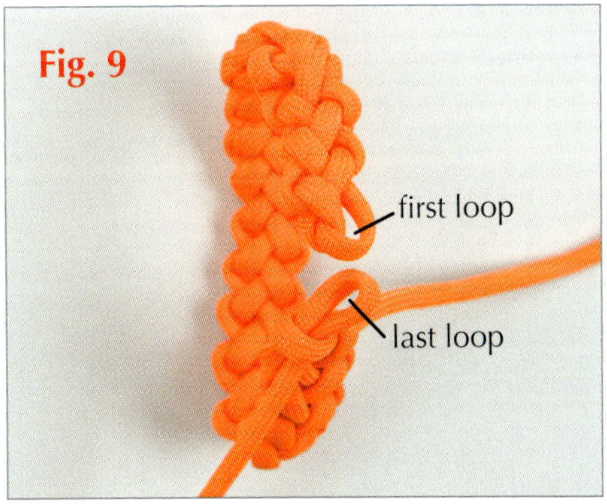

Fig. 10

8. Insert the non-sliding cord through the loop. Pull on both cord ends to tighten the knot ***(Fig. 11)***. **Trim and Finish** the ends *(page 5)*.

Fig. 11

STITCHED SOLOMAN BAR KNOT

TWO COLOR BRACELET WITH LOOP AND KNOT

Shown in red and white on page 34.

SHOPPING LIST

- ☐ 550 paracord – one 18' hank **each** of two colors
- ☐ utility scissors
- ☐ tape measure, ruler, or yardstick
- ☐ craft glue
- ☐ masking, painter's, or duct tape

***Tip:** Taping down the top loop and the standing cord ends makes it easier to tie knots around the standing cords.*

1. Cut an 11' length of cord for the working cords and a 5' length of cord for the standing cords.

2. Fold the standing cord in half and center it on the working cord ***(Fig. 1)***.

Fig. 1

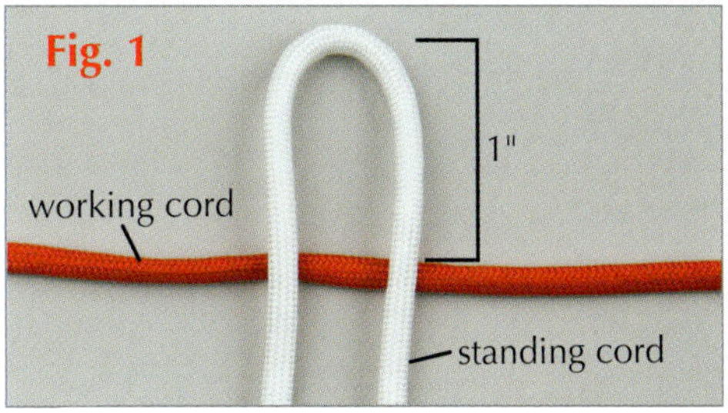

3. Knot the working cord onto the standing cord as shown in **Fig. 2**; pull the working cords to tighten.

Fig. 2

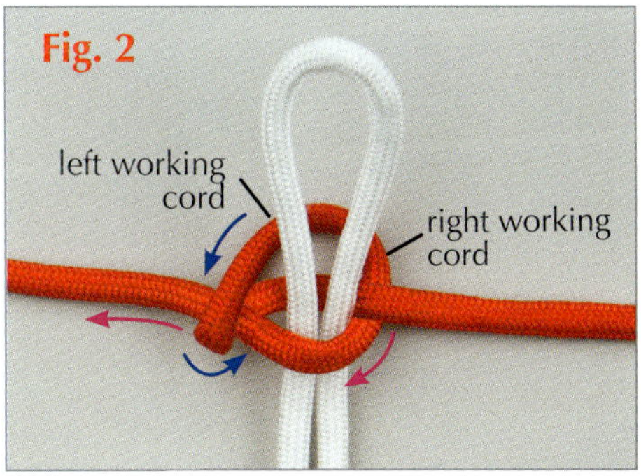

Continued on page 36.

Stitched Solomon Bar Knot continued.

4. Bring the left working cord between the standing cords and the right working cord behind the standing cords. Bring the working cord ends through the side loops ***(Fig. 3)***; tighten.

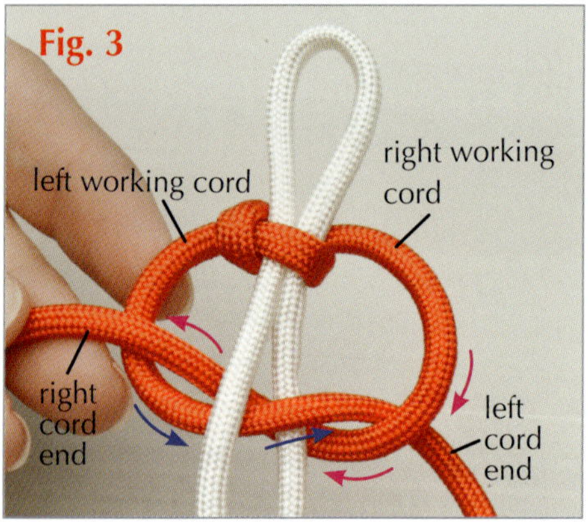

5. Bring the right working cord between the standing cords and the left working cord behind the standing cords. Bring the working cord ends through the side loops ***(Fig. 4)***; tighten.

6. Repeat Steps 4-5 ***(Fig. 5)***, stopping when the knotted section is 1" short of your finished bracelet size.

7. On the wrong side, thread the working cord ends under the last knot ***(Fig. 6)***; tighten. **Trim and Finish** *(page 5)* the ends.

8. Use the standing cords to make a **Diamond Knot** *(pages 46-48)*.

ONE COLOR BRACELET WITH BUCKLE

Shown in rainbow on page 34.

SHOPPING LIST

- ☐ 550 paracord – one 18' hank
- ☐ side-release buckle
- ☐ utility scissors
- ☐ craft glue
- ☐ tape measure, ruler, or yardstick
- ☐ masking, painter's, or duct tape

***Tip:** Taping down the top and bottom buckle makes it easier to tie knots around the standing cords.*

1. Fold the cord in half and insert the loop through one buckle piece from front to back. Bring the cords through the loop ***(Fig. 7)***; pull to tighten ***(Fig. 8)***.

Fig. 7

Fig. 8

2. Thread the cord ends through the remaining buckle piece from front to back and position the buckle at your finished bracelet size ***(Fig. 9)***.

Fig. 9

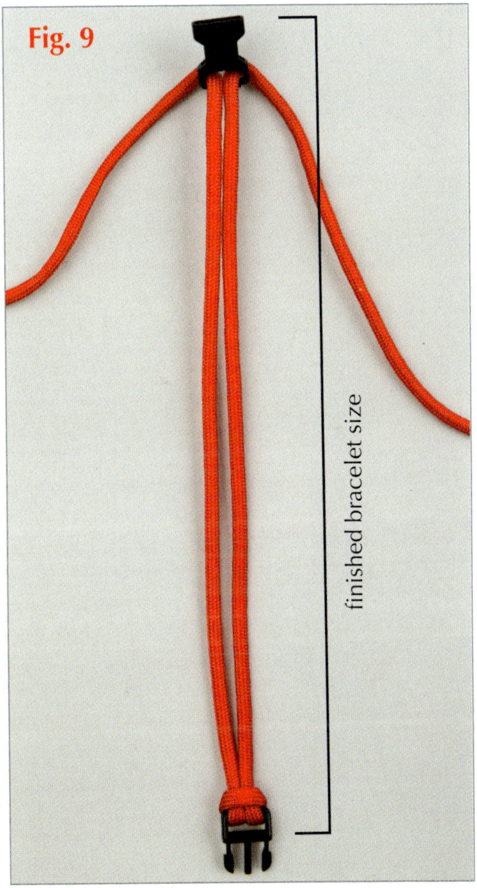

3. Bring the left working cord over the standing cords and behind the right working cord. Bring the right working cord behind the standing cords and over the left working cord ***(Fig. 10)***; tighten.

Fig. 10

4. Repeat Steps 4-5 of **One Color Bracelet with Loop And Knot,** *(page 36)*, until you reach the beginning buckle.

5. Referring to ***Fig. 6, page 37***, thread the working cord ends under the last knot; tighten. **Trim and Finish** *(page 5)* the ends.

RAISING THE BAR KNOT

TWO COLOR BRACELET WITH LOOP AND KNOT

Shown in pink and black on page 40.

SHOPPING LIST

- ☐ 550 paracord – one 18' hank **each** of two colors
- ☐ utility scissors
- ☐ tape measure, ruler, or yardstick
- ☐ craft glue
- ☐ masking, painter's, or duct tape

Tip: *Taping down the top loop and the standing cord ends makes it easier to tie knots around the standing cords.*

1. Fold one cord in half and center it on the second cord.

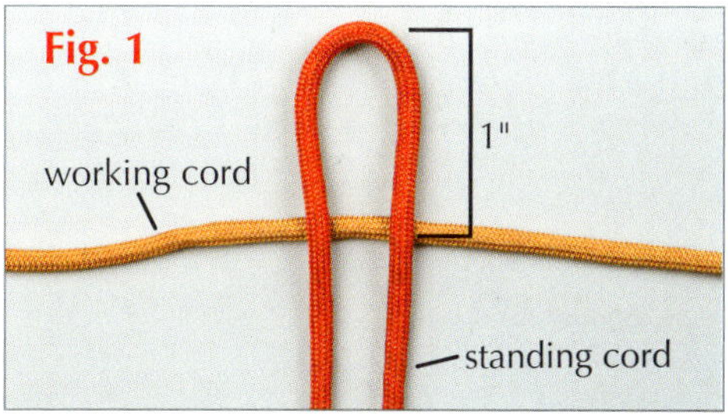

Continued on page 42.

Raising The Bar Knot continued.

2. Knot the working cord onto the stranding cord as shown in **Fig. 2**; pull the working cords to tighten. Turn cords over so the knot is on the top.

Fig. 2

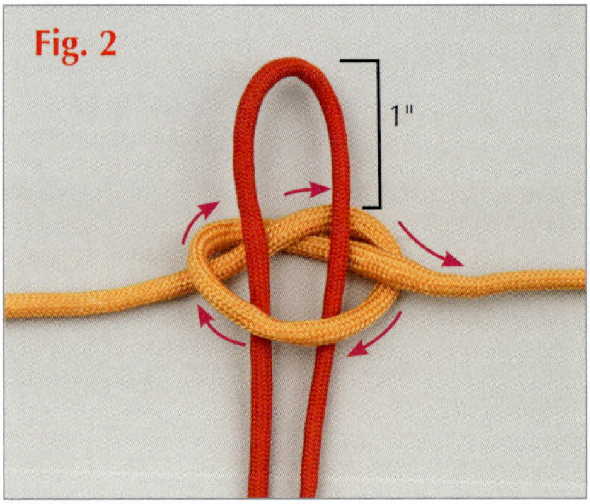

Fig. 3

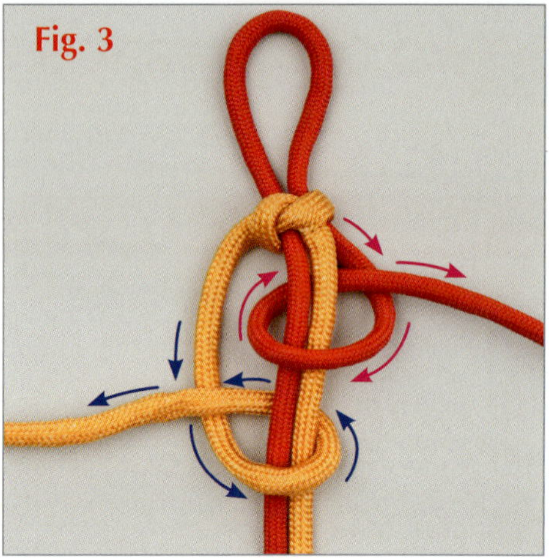

3. Using one cord of each color as the working cords, wrap the right and then the left working cords around the standing cords ***(Fig. 3)***; tighten ***(Fig. 4)***.

Fig. 4

4. Alternating right and left cords, repeat Step 3 until the knotted section is 1" short of your finished bracelet size ***(Figs. 5-6)***.

Fig. 5

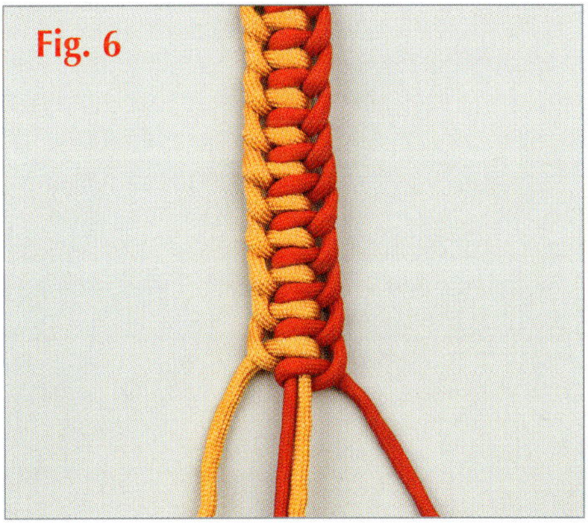
Fig. 6

5. On the wrong side, thread the working cords under the last knot ***(Fig. 7)***; tighten. **Trim and Finish** *(page 5)* the ends.

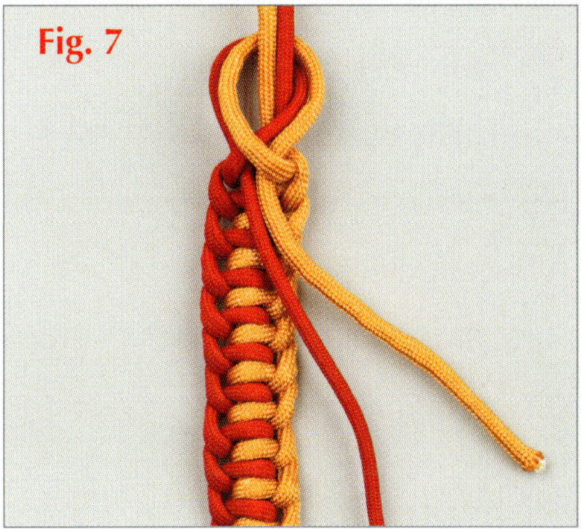
Fig. 7

6. Use the standing cords to make a **Diamond Knot** *(pages 46-48)*.

TWO COLOR BRACELET WITH BUCKLE

Shown in gold and green on page 40.

SHOPPING LIST

- ☐ 550 paracord – one 18' hank **each** of two colors
- ☐ side-release buckle
- ☐ utility scissors
- ☐ tape measure, ruler, or yardstick
- ☐ craft glue
- ☐ masking, painter's, or duct tape

***Tip:** Taping down the top and bottom buckle makes it easier to tie knots around the standing cords.*

1. Fold both cords in half and insert one cord through each buckle opening from front to back ***(Fig. 8)***.

Fig. 8

2. Bring all four cord ends through both loops ***(Fig. 9)***; pull the cords to tighten ***(Fig. 10)***.

Fig. 9

Fig. 10

3. Follow Steps 3-4 of **Two Color Bracelet with Loop And Knot** *(pages 42-43)* to tie a series of **Raising The Bar** knots, stopping 1" short of your finished bracelet size.

4. Thread all four cord ends through the remaining buckle piece from front to back.

5. On the wrong side, thread the standing cord ends under the last knot; **Trim and Finish** *(page 5)* the cord ends. Repeat to secure the working cord ends under the next-to-last knot ***(Fig. 11)***.

Fig. 11

HOW TO TIE A DIAMOND KNOT

A Diamond Knot makes a firm, round ball that is used for all bracelets that close with a loop and knot.

Note: *When tying a Diamond Knot, the right cord is always the right cord (shown in green) and the left cord is always the left cord (shown in red) even if they move to the opposite side of the knot. The numbers in () match the numbers on the Figs. where the cords go over or under each other. The placement for a Diamond Knot is approximately 1" from the end of your bracelet.*

1. Make a loop in the left cord. Bring the right cord behind the loop and over the left cord ***(Fig. 1)***.

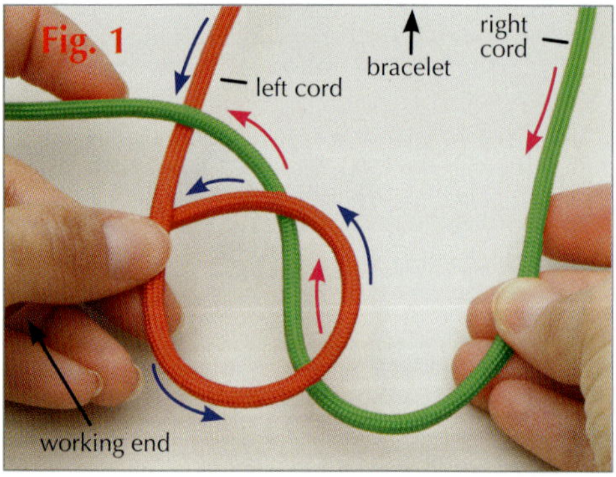

2. Bring the right cord under the left cord working end (1), over the bottom of the loop of the left cord (2), and under the top of the loop of the right cord (3), forming a diamond in the center of the loops ***(Fig. 2)***.

Fig. 2

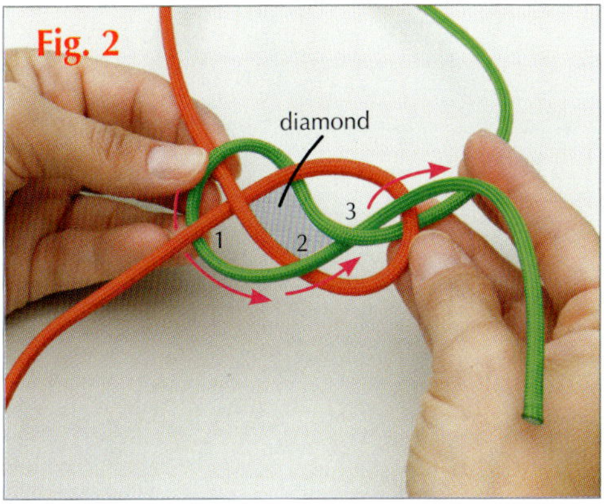

3. Bring the left working end around the top of the knot ***(Fig. 3)***, under all the loops, and through the diamond from the back to the front. Bring the right working end around the bottom of the knot ***(Fig. 4)***, under all the loops, and through the diamond from the back to the front ***(Fig. 5)***.

Fig. 3

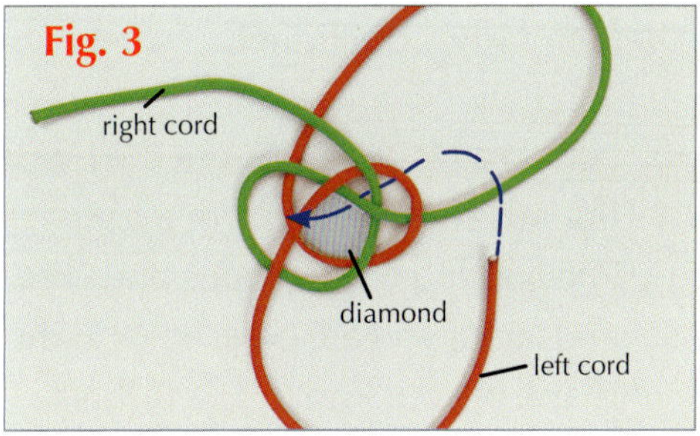

Fig. 4

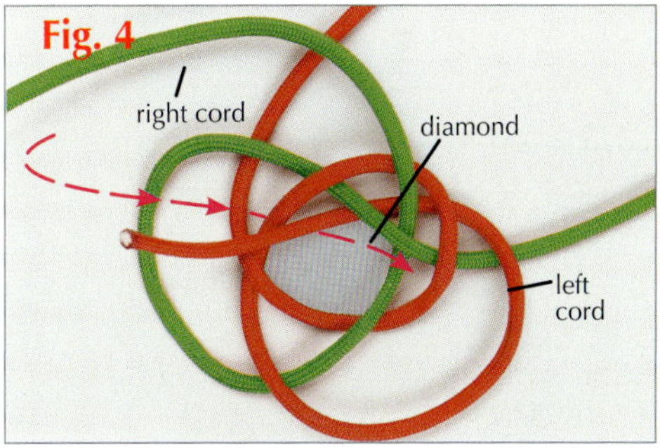

Fig. 5

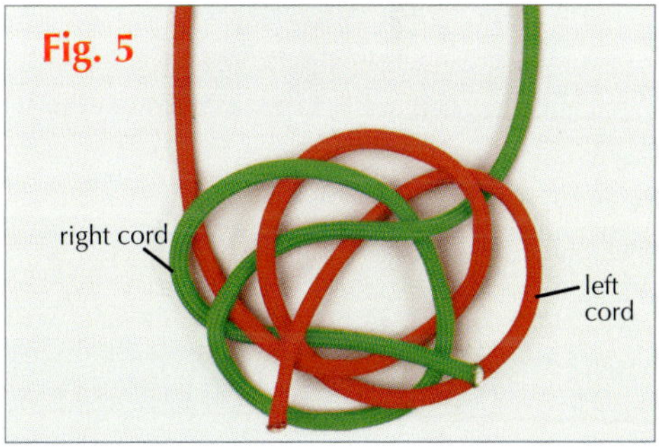

Continued on page 48.

Diamond Knot continued.

4. Pull on all four cords until the loops tighten and start to form a ball. Pull and tug on the loops and cord ends until you are pleased with the shape of your knot ***(Figs. 6-8)***.

5. **Trim and Finish** *(page 5)* the ends ***(Fig. 8)***.

Fig. 7

Fig. 6

Fig. 8

We have made every effort to ensure that these instructions are accurate and complete. We cannot, however, be responsible for human error, typographical mistakes, or variations in individual work.